ACKNOWLEDGEMENTS

The Author gratefully acknowledges the assistance of the following:—

James Stevens-Cox, Esq., F.S.A., St. Peter Port, Guernsey.

Alan Willis, Esq., Hon Ceramics Adviser to the Russell Cotes Museum, Bournemouth, for photographic work.

Sean McCrum, Esq., The Ulster Museum, Belfast.

Cecil Whitfield, Esq., for photographic work of the Parkfield Collection.

Mrs. Alison Farrell for typewriting.

Mrs. J. M. Sweet, M.A., B.Litt., for proof reading.

Richard Beck, Esq., B.Sc., for photographic work.

J. V. G. Mallet, Esq., Keeper of Ceramics, Victoria and Albert Museum.

The Trustees of the Victoria and Albert Museum, (V. & A. in text) South Kensington, for permission to reproduce photographs of their Belleek Collection.

The Trustees of the Ulster Museum for permission to reproduce photographs of their Belleek Collection.

The Trustees of the Merseyside County Museum for permission to reproduce photographs of sections from their Catalogue of Belleek for 1923.

The Keepers of the Ceramic Departments of the Museums of Stoke-on-Trent, Birmingham and Leicester.

For assistance with the section on American Belleek the Author gratefully acknowledges the following:—

Mr. Ed Grusheski, Department of Cultural History, New Jersey State Museum, Trenton, New Jersey, U.S.A.

Mrs. Frances Gruber Safford, Metropolitan Museum of Art, New York, U.S.A.

Trustees of the Du Pont Winterthur Museum, U.S.A.

University Press of Virginia, Charlottesville, U.S.A.

Anna Reilly, and the publishers of "The Spinning Wheel", Milwaukee, U.S.A.

James Mitchell, Director of the William Penn Memorial Museum, Harrisburg, Pennsylvania, U.S.A.

Fig. 1
"The Aberdeen Vase." 4th mark in black. Height 5½in. Still in production today with 5th mark. Parkfield Collection.

ISBN 0 85694 150 6

BELLEEK PORCELAIN AND POTTERY

A HANDBOOK FOR THE COLLECTOR

BY

G. M. SMITH

25 ILLUSTRATIONS

Toucan Press

Mount Durand, St. Peter Port,

Guernsey, C.I., via Britain.

1979

THE AUTHOR

Gerald Morley Smith was born in 1926, educated at Wycliffe College, and lives in the New Forest. He is a director of one of the largest meat wholesaling companies in the country and of the only remaining mill within the City of Salisbury. His interests outside of his business are, **inter alia,** music, cricket and Belleek porcelain which he has been enthusiastically collecting and studying for over twenty years.

For my wife, Bunnie, who first suggested this little book.

FOREWORD

"He who would search for pearls must dive below." Dryden.

This book is intended as a companionable guide for collectors of Belleek. It is not, however, in any sense an expert textbook, but rather an informal, illustrated monograph. The reasons for the appeal of Belleek are not hard to find, and most collectors when asked what first drew them to it would say, not necessarily in this order, that it was the fascinating designs, the eggshell thinness, the glaze and the soft colours. But there is another reason that has been of paramount importance in directing people's interest to Belleek, a reason that still holds, and that is cost. For the hard pressed British taxpayer with a family and all the problems of keeping solvent has only limited opportunities to invest in works of art, fine porcelain or good furniture.

One brand of porcelain that for some years has been undervalued, is Belleek. The fact of its moderate cost has meant that collectors of modest means have been able to build fine collections of this delightful Irish porcelain, without subsiding into bankruptcy. They now see their collections valued at two or three times the price they paid for it a few years ago.

To the confirmed Belleek lover and collector the appeal is clear, but it would be wrong to pretend that it is to everybody's taste. The shapes, glaze colours and character of Belleek which is unique in the field of porcelain, produce strong reactions. It would seem to the writer that there are few people indifferent to Belleek. You are for it or you are not. The shapes fascinate or they irritate, the colours please or they bore, the translucent eggshell-thin paste of Belleek charms and delights, or it may appear trivial and flimsy.

It is hoped that the reader who is not already a Belleek collector will come to love this rare, delicate, quirky, idiosyncratic parian ware from Fermanagh and that he will seek fine examples of it, display them in his drawing room, in an elegant cabinet, and share his enjoyment with friends of a similar taste.

THE EARLY DAYS

In 1857 Queen Victoria had been on the throne for some twenty years, Lord Palmerston was Prime Minister and Abraham Lincoln was soon to become President of the United States. In the village of Broadheath near Worcester Sir Edward Elgar was born. The Empire was intact and fairly obedient, with the exception of a mighty mutiny in India. The Industrial Revolution was in full spate, and the middle classes were thrusting to be upper middle class, and a whole new enthusiasm was afoot in building fine houses and filling them with pictures, furniture and porcelain. In that same year in Fermanagh, Ireland, a porcelain factory was established in the village of Belleek on the banks of the River Erne.

A Captain Bloomfield owned an estate which included the village of Belleek and he had the foresight to have tested the quality of large deposits of felspar on his land. The distinguished Dublin architect, Robert Armstrong (Fig. 3) was approached and he took samples of the Irish felspar to Kerr at Worcester, where it was tried with Cornish china clay and found after test firings to produce excellent results.

Armstrong saw the possibility of manufacturing pottery and although artistic, talented, and capable of brilliant original ideas, he was not a wealthy man and was only able to proceed with the development of the Irish felspar with the help of his friend, David McBirney, who had capital. The two men formed a partnership which, at first, traded as D. McBirney & Co., and later as the Belleek Pottery Co.

Not only was Armstrong farsighted enough to see the possibilities of Belleek, he designed and built the factory. The machinery installed was to his specification, and the copious local water supply of the River Erne was harnessed to provide power for the new works, also engineered by Armstrong.

At first some seventy people were employed at the new factory, (Fig. 2) a valuable source of income in the West of Ireland in the middle of the 19th century, only twelve years after the dire ravages of the potato famines. The factory turned out excellent quality everyday ware, but the Belleek which we know today was the result of the purchase from the French Chemist Briancon of his patented pearl-like glazing process. This was a mixture of oil of lavender, salts of bismuth and resin and produced the now famous nacreous glaze.

Although a great variety of fine china has been produced at Belleek since the foundation in 1857, to the casual porcelain collector the name immediately brings to mind the eggshell thin ware, examples of which appear illustrated in this book. This exceptional thinness is produced by pouring the slip into plaster of Paris moulds which, being very porous, absorb moisture and reduces the thickness of the porcelain by between 25 and 33%. When glazed this delicate ware is remarkably tough, though hardly everyday china.

The skill required for the production of the eggshell china came from Goss's works; several of his men worked at Belleek for some years led by William Bromley who is credited with the final perfection of the parian ware. The eggshell china, among the finest in the world, and the equal of Dresden, was produced together with a great variety of other wares, statues, tableware and decorative china. The parian body was often tinted with soft colours before the iridescent glazing, producing a wholly delightful effect. Concurrent with the production of the marvellous new nacreous porcelain the works turned out a steady stream of excellent granite ware and everyday domestic ware, even telephone wire insulators.

From its earliest days, Belleek proceiain has been much sought after especially in the United States and Great Britain. That is still so today. Large orders were placed with the works by famous shops including Robinson and Cleaver of Belfast. In the Parkfield Collection there is a cup and saucer with the mark combined with that of the name of the shop (Fig. 21).

By the 1880's the number employed at Belleek, including apprentices, was around 200, which shows how well the wares from the factory had appealed to the Victorian public, a public supposedly only capable of liking massive furniture and over-ornate buildings. Of course some Belleek is unashamedly Victorian (and why not?) and perhaps not quite to the taste of the more severely aesthetic, but even these lofty souls will grant that the pieces are beautifully made and that the glaze is unique.

In 1883 the partners died; the artistic drive of Armstrong was lost, but his designs and patterns remain to the present day. The factory had a succession of owners and as is so often the case following a founder's death, a few rather troubled periods lay ahead.

THE FACTORY TODAY

To visit the Belleek establishment is an experience to be remembered for all time, for this is no ordinary factory in which workpeople labour away with frequent glances at the clock. Indeed, there appear to be no workpeople, only craftsmen and women, and many are young people just out of school.

A tradition exists at Belleek of children following their parents, and this continuity produces a rare atmosphere of dedication which in no small way is reflected in the exquisite china leaving the factory today. Armstrong's fine building remains, handsome and sound, its pitch pine roof timbers now out of sight above new ceilings, and in the building the skills which produce the world-famous wares are now combined with the latest machinery. But there is nothing mechanical about the production of Belleek parian china other than that which it is sensible to mechanise, such as grinding and the new wood chip vibrating machine for removing particles after the first firing.

The local felspar is now exhausted, and the source of the present felspar is Norway. The china clay still comes from Fowey, in Cornwall. Little else has changed, the glaze no longer contains the dangerous red lead in use for some years prior to the 1950's, but now consists of white lead, borax and flint.

The delicate strands for the basket-making are produced exactly as in the old days, by extrusion. Great pressure is exerted on the paste by means of iron presses hand turned, and the baskets are made by one craftsman throughout. There is no production line at Belleek! The fruit basket takes three days to make, and costs over £200.00 (See Fig. 14).

Many of the original designs are in current production and apart from the new mark and rather creamier paste it would be difficult to see the difference from pieces over 100 years old; certainly the quality and beauty of the porcelain is unchanged. An innovation is the gilding of the edges of some tea services, producing a most beautiful effect.

The basket work is still identified by the strip mark impressed "Belleek Fermanagh", and even this is put on by the craftsman making it. The usual transfer mark is put on between the second and third firings, which are carried out in modern electric kilns at 1,200°C at the first firing, lasting 18 hours, 950°C at the second firing lasting 12 hours, and the final and third firing at 600°C for 6 hours (Fig. 5).

Throughout the factory, as one proceeds from one department to another, one is met with the same scene. People young, and not so young, sitting at wooden benches before high windows working mostly in good natural light with a dedication and concentration not too common in this plastic age, a work-force approaching 200 people under the enlightened direction of the O'Neill family. Our guide on our recent visit had nearly 40 years service at Belleek and he said this was far from being a record (Fig. 10).

Following the disaster of the deaths of both Armstrong and McBirney, the factory was run by a local group of businessmen, but they clearly lacked the vision of Armstrong, and that combined with the catastrophe of the First World War, and the loss of their export business led to the failure of the pottery by 1918. For a business of any size to fail in Ireland in an area beset with unemployment, was a total disaster. But the Grandfather of Mr. S. J. O'Neill (who very kindly received the author on a recent visit), in conjunction with a few business associates, was responsible for restarting the pottery and leading it to its present pre-eminent position in the world of fine ceramic ware.

The factory survived the Second World War, the production being confined to plain and practical goods for the home market, a far cry from its traditional delicate china made for a discerning home and export market.

This then in brief is the story of Belleek, a story of tradition, of utter painstaking care and of dedication, by management and craftsmen, from Robert Armstrong in 1857 to S. J. O'Neill in 1978.

Truly could the artists at Belleek claim that they maintain today all that is best in Britain's ceramic art, and in Belleek in Western Ireland these skills are second to none.

THE BELLEEK PATTERNS

Illustrated in this book are photographs of Belleek from the Author's Parkfield Collection, the Victoria and Albert Museum and the Ulster Museum, the latter two by kind permission of the Trustees, and they all illustrate better than words the very characteristic designs and models which are unique to Belleek.

Robert Armstrong, one of the joint founders of the factory, was a very distinguished architect and friend of Kerr at Worcester, and he was responsible for many of the designs. So too was his wife who enjoyed a reputation as a landscape painter of some note. Gallimore, seconded from the Goss works, was also a very active modeller for Belleek and is credited with about five hundred designs and the introduction of the shell patterns. Another native of Stoke, Henshall, is credited with the introduction of the basket weaving and applied flower designs (see S. McCrum's The Belleek Pottery, Ulster Museum Publication I88). Henshall was working at Belleek for nearly forty years until the turn of the century, which illustrates still further the association between Belleek and Worcester which extended over many years.

Two other designers at Belleek were young students of Gallimore named James Cleary and Michael Maguire; they continued Gallimore's naturalistic models as well as introducing models of their own. It is not possible to say with certainty who of the several modellers at Belleek was responsible for which piece, as they were not signed.

All the designs are so characteristic of Belleek as to be impossible to con-

Fig. 2

The original factory on an island surrounded by the River Erme. Armstrong harnessed the Erne to provide power for his new factory.

Fig. 3

Robert Armstrong (died 1884). From a photograph in the Pottery Gazette of 1906.

fuse with any other porcelains, British or Continental. As one studies and acquires Belleek a feel for it develops which can be of much comfort to the amateur.

It might even be said that through much Belleek runs a "leitmotiv" as is the case with so much 19th Century music. The connection is there clearly, a sense of order and a seeking after excellence, yet with a strong romantic warmth which until a few years ago it was fashionable to despise, but no longer.

THE MARKS

For the amateur porcelain collector, marks can be a minefield and can exercise the minds of even skilled ceramic experts. Some wares are left unmarked, which could be the case when a family ordered a complete dinner service, tea service and other pieces bearing arms, crests or family mottoes. The Worcester factory marks alone cover ten pages in J. P. Cushion's Pocket Book of British Ceramic Marks (Faber & Faber), a very necessary book for any porcelain collector. So the field is wide and fraught with difficulties and pitfalls, not the least of which was the pirating of other makers' marks, particularly of Meissen.

In the case of Belleek, the collector has little to fear; the subject of course is much simpler than Worcester or Spode and the factory of more recent founding.

Fraudulent marks would not be difficult for any student of Belleek to spot as there is little problem with identifying them. The body, glaze, designs, all are too characteristic to confuse with any other porcelain.

Collectors may have been puzzled at the scant attention given to Belleek and its marks by such authorities as Goddard and Cushion, who show only two marks in the latest edition of the pocket book.

There are in fact six marks, including the impressed strip mark "Belleek Co. Fermanagh" which was fired on the basketwork pieces, it being impossible to use the usual printed mark on the finely woven porcelain. The sequence of the familiar hound, harp and tower mark is as follows: —

The First Mark (Fig. 4) printed usually in black (occasionally in red, blue grey etc.) comprised the hound, harp and tower and was the smallest mark to come from the factory, measuring little more than half an inch in width and height. This mark was current from the founding in 1857 until about 1865.

The Second Mark (Fig. 4) first appeared around 1865 and is nearly twice the size of the First Mark with the hound filled in. This mark was printed in dark brown, green or blue. The coloured mark was current until about 1870 when it became black.

The Third Mark (Fig. 4) is rare and comprises a harp surmounted by a crown, and was usually impressed. This mark was concurrently used with the First and Second Marks and continued until the mid-1890's.

The Fourth Mark (Fig. 4) first appeared in 1891 with a scroll bearing the name "Co. Fermanagh Ireland" beneath the usual "hound, tower and harp mark". This addition was required by the American McKinley tariff act and the British Merchandise act which made the naming of the country of manufacture compulsory. It was printed in black.

The Fifth Mark (Fig. 4) superceded the Fourth Mark in 1926, was printed in black and with the trade name and number "0857". This mark changed to green in 1947 and modern post-1955 Belleek bears an (R.) mark showing that it is a registered Trade Mark of the United States.

Fig. 4
No. 1 First Mark, No. 2 Second Mark, No. 3 Third Mark, No. 4 Fourth Mark, No. 5 Fifth Mark. Bottom right hand; mark with name "Robinson and Cleaver" added
See text page 10 for full details of these marks.

The Sixth or Strip Mark (Fig. 5) spans the whole period of the pottery's activity and consists of one or two strips with the words "Belleek Co. Fermanagh" impressed and fired invariably on the base of the piece.

One other point of interest with Belleek (and other porcelain) is the use of the Patent Office Registration Mark usually called the Diamond Mark which was in use from 1842 until 1883. This mark showed that the design was registered with the Patent Office. Illustrated is a particularly fine mark on a cup and saucer of the Second Period from the author's Parkfield Collection (Fig. 6) which shows the date of registration of the design as 22nd February 1869. The date of manufacture would have been 1869 or a year or so later.

The interpretation of Patent Office Marks is expounded with great clarity in J. P. Cushion's "Pocket Book of Ceramic Marks" (Faber and Faber). It is not reproduced here as Diamond Marks are not very common on Belleek, but for an interpretation of this particular mark see Fig. 6.

So there it is, the entire sequence of six marks with really only four that are commonly found (Nos. 1, 2, 4 and 5).

DISPLAY AND CARE

Belleek should be kept in glazed cabinets and well lit, either by direct light from windows or with electric lighting fitted to the inside of the cabinet. The choice of cabinet is entirely a matter of taste, but choose cabinets with large clear glass panels so that your collection is clearly visible. Background is rather important; for instance a pale green or other neutral shade will not show your collection to best advantage. A deep red, green or brown velvet lined cabinet is ideal, contrasting well with the delicate variations of pearl and cream found in Belleek.

Make an effort to display your collection with thought, placing the pieces well apart, as a crowded shelf or cabinet is not very attractive. Place large pieces behind smaller pieces and arrange so as to achieve a pleasing ensemble.

If you display your Belleek on shelves or table tops the hazards are great. Damage is always probable and the intricate designs of many pieces will collect dust, with consequent dulling of the glaze.

Wash Belleek as you would any fine china in warm soapy water. The more intricate pieces you will not be able to wipe dry, so rinse them in clear water before drying with a hair dryer. Never scrub china and take care not to erase the printed marks, which may well be unglazed on the base of the piece.

It is common for Belleek to become stained in corners and folds; particularly is this so with vases which have been used for flowers. Remove the stains with a solution of household bleach and water and allow it to stand until the stain has gone. It may need a little gentle rubbing with a soft bristled brush if the staining is particularly tenacious.

Fig. 5

Strip mark in porcelain fired on to base of Belleek woven basket, bearing the words "Belleek, Fermanagh" (see text p. 12 for details).

Fig. 6

Diamond or registry mark on base of Belleek cup, second period. Explanation mark—clockwise from top, IV=class (i.e. porcelain), 22=Day, H=year (1869), G=month (Feb.), II=parcel number. Photographs of Figs. 5 and 6 by Cecil Whitfield.

VALUES

One of the greatest problems facing the collector of antiquities of any kind during the period since the end of the last war has been the steady and at times meteoric increase in prices. As already mentioned, this has been caused by inflation and the consequent cheapening of money, hence more of this poor quality money is needed to buy things.

Belleek, in common with all fine porcelain has increased sharply in price, but not yet to a point where the wretched taxpayer is forced to window shop and nothing else. Clearly it is not possible for one to give firm values, but fine quality pieces of middle and late period Belleek can sometimes be bought for a few pounds but some of the finest examples of the early period could cost £200 or more. At the time of writing (1976) the author has recently purchased a very fine First Mark cup and saucer for £15 and the perfect Fourth Mark Thistle Vase for £40 (Fig. 23).

Cream jugs can be bought for about £7 to £10. That these prices are modest is clear, but they illustrate the point that Belleek is well within the range of the porcelain lover with modest funds and that means most of us. When you decide to become a collector of antique porcelain you can be either a vertical or a horizontal collector.

If you are a vertical collector you just collect, for example, jugs. Jugs of all periods from the earliest Staffordshire to the best 20th Century, and nothing but jugs. People have been known to make large collections of chamber pots, an even more limiting activity.

But the horizontal collector collects, for instance, Belleek: all periods and many different patterns and pieces, and the writer suggests, gets much more fun in his collecting. If you are a confirmed Belleek collector it would not be possible to be also a vertical collector. How could you select from your trustworthy antique dealer friend an exquisite First Mark teapot (Fig. 18), and pass over without a second thought the quite delightful little jardiniere alongside it? (Fig. 20). Of course you could not, so you are a horizontal collector!

So far that very important person in your life, the antique dealer, has not been mentioned, and this is because he is so important and requires some close attention. My collecting of Belleek would have been nearly impossible without the guidance and help of a particular dealer friend, who has found for me some of the best pieces in the Parkfield Collection.

There are those who think they will do well on their own, who resent the possibility that the dealer might make a profit out of them. Oddly enough, these same people probably eat in restaurants and buy clothes and motor cars, but they are their own D.I.Y. antique experts. Good luck to them.

The good antique dealer is more than worthy of his hire, particularly if his showrooms are laid out as are those of Mr. Ray Taylor at Gordleton Mill Antiques near Lymington, in the author's view quite the ideal for the collector with a few pounds to spend, or a few hundred. Beware of the dealer where nothing is priced, but each piece of porcelain, each chair and picture has a wretched little tag on it in code, which only the dealer can interpret. At Gordleton Mill everything is clearly priced and even more helpful for the timid ignoramous, described.

A **good** antique dealer should be your right arm as a collector. Consult him regularly; he will give you excellent advice, point out tiny flaws in the fragile Belleek cup for which you have fallen and show you another one slightly dearer that is perfect. When you are known to a dealer he will keep his eye open for pieces he thinks might appeal to you when he attends sales or buys privately. You are busy about your business, so do not begrudge the dealer his just reward for standing for hours in cold sale rooms and then cleaning and exhibiting his purchases in the hope that he will sell them, perhaps within days, or in a year's time.

The dedicated Belleek collector must search endlessly for good pieces; stop at all antique shops and keep an eye on the house contents for sale columns in the local paper as well as ceramic sales. Only thus will he get a true idea of the market values, and form a collection. Be selective, never buy any piece of porcelain, be it Belleek or Spode, Worcester or Caughley, unless you like it and do not buy it **because** it is Belleek. In the Parkfield Collection are only pieces that were chosen for their appeal to the author, as not every single piece to leave Fermanagh is to the taste of every collector.

My sole purchase in Ireland was a pair of pleasant Fourth Mark cream jugs from the then Mayor of Waterford, who has a shop on the quayside street in the town centre. The good Mayor observed as he wrapped up my modest purchase: "Tis a mystery where all the Belleek is gone to". Gone it certainly had.

The vexed question of damaged or flawed antique porcelain deserves a word and particularly so in the case of Belleek which is so fine. Do not reject out of hand a slightly damaged piece. Your dealer will know it is damaged and will have priced it accordingly at a lesser figure than for a perfect piece. If the piece is interesting or rare add it to your collection; it will take a close inspection to reveal the damage which I am assuming is small. If the dealer has by some chance not spotted the damage, point it out and make an offer for the piece. A little horse trading offends nobody except the most stuffy dealers. If in the future you find a perfect specimen, you can always trade out the imperfect piece if it offends you and it will have appreciated in value along with the perfect items of your collection.

Try to make your collection as representative as possible with pieces from all five periods including a piece or two of the beautiful new ware leaving the factory today. In the Parkfield Collection there are two or three modern pieces including the handsome mug illustrated (Fig. 25).

In addition to seeking pieces from all periods, make the collection, varied with as many designs as you can afford. Include examples of the marvellous basket ware, (Fig. 14) plates, statuary, cups and saucers and teapots. The variety is great, so aim to make your collection representative of designs as well as periods.

AMERICAN BELLEEK

No guide to Belleek would be truly complete without a section on American "Belleek" much of which was produced in the Trenton area during the last decade of the 19th Century and the first decade of this century. This American Belleek became an excellent unofficial copy of the original Irish Belleek.

To find American Belleek in the British Isles is unusual. With the Irish factory near at hand what reason could there be for large imports other than low prices? Wages and costs of materials in the thriving United States would not be lower than in the largely depressed West of Ireland, but some American Belleek did reach this country and two identical and perfect shell bowls are in the Parkfield Collection (Fig. 9).

Clearly there are differences between the Irish and the American Belleek, the body of the author's two pieces is whiter than the Irish variety, although just as finely cast and glazed.

Naturalistic models were widely used by the American factories, whether imported from the home works or copied is not known, but most probably they were pirated designs. The distinctive nacreous glaze was also mastered in time by Ott and Brewer, the makers of the Parkfield pieces.

The introduction of Belleek into the United States was undertaken by the Ott and Brewer Company of Trenton, New Jersey, Irish immigrants encouraging production, indeed Irish names crop up regularly among the potters and designers responsible for its production. It was not a case of the original factory starting American subsidiaries, on the contrary the American production interfered with the exports of the home factory.

Mr. Ed Grusheski, Curator of Cultural History at the New Jersey State Museum writes, "Ott and Brewer first introduced "Belleek" into the U.S. in 1883 with the assistance of William Bromley Sr., who brought over the "secret process" from Belleek to Ott and Brewer. Bromley was quickly lured away by the rival potter, Willets, at Trenton. This firm produced Belleek in great quantities and production of the fashionable porcelain body mushroomed". Set against the economic background of the United States at the end of the 19th Century and the stream of Irish immigrants arriving in the Eastern States it is easy to see how this mushrooming took place. A young vigorous country unhampered by restrictive government interference and an eager homesick flood of customers anxious for reminders of home, combined to produce a ready market for this unique Irish porcelain.

The body was very similar, the models were like original Belleek and the glaze was as good as the home product (in the case of the best Ott and Brewer ware, but not of all the Trenton makers). Mr. Grusheski continues, "Between 1883 and 1910 at least 8 Trenton factories produced a Belleek body of one kind or another. Moreover, potters familiar with the process left Trenton for Ohio to produce Belleek there. Admittedly the further away one goes in time and space from Ott and Brewer Belleek the less the American bodies resemble the Irish. In the New Jersey State Museum we have examples of Belleek from 6 of the Trenton factories". With potteries springing up, moving, and closing down, it can be seen that any historian tackling this subject is faced with daunting problems. Indeed Grusheski states that it has never been fully recorded.

Some points of interest can be gleaned from an article by Anna Reilly in the June 1952 edition of "The Spinning Wheel", entitled "American Belleek, the Porcelain of Eire from the Banks of the Delaware River". (The Belleek factory is of course now in Northern Ireland, but its products are and have always been regarded as a National treasure, with no dreary political boundaries affecting its popularity). Anna Reilly writes, "When Irish Belleek was exhibited at the Philadelphia Centennial in 1876 it caused such a sensation that many potters interested in producing porcelain of equal quality began to do something about it. Belleek was first manufactured in this country in Trenton and although a number of potteries in the area attempted production the wares of some of them did not reach the market, partly because of shortage of funds to carry out the manufacture of this intricate porcelain".

Among factories producing Belleek in the Trenton area around the turn of the Century were the following:—

1. The Etruria Pottery, founded in 1863 by Bloor Ott and Booth and operated by the Ott and Brewer Company. The President, John Brewer, was assisted at first by William Bromley Jr. (from Belleek) in early trials for Belleek production but with little success. It was not until 1883 when Bromley Senior arrived with other skilled potters that the fine quality eggshell porcelain was made, and in 1884 the first American Belleek came on to the market. Ornamental and household pieces were made, light and delicate tea and coffee services. The mark was a crown and sword with crescent from 1876 to 1882 (see Fig. 7) and from 1883 to 1892 the crescent mark (see Fig. 8).

2. The Cook Company, successors to Ott and Brewer in 1894, continued the familiar Belleek models. Mark, three feathers and the word "Etruria" beneath.

3. The Delaware Pottery. Founded in about 1886 by T. Donnelly, an employee from the Irish Belleek factory. Very high quality Belleek produced comparable with the original Irish ware. Not a financial success, Mark unknown.

4. The Willits Manufacturing Company. In 1879 the three Willit brothers bought an existing pottery and began to produce Belleek. It was to this works that William Bromley Sr. defected from Ott and Brewer, and began training the Willit potters in the art of Belleek production. Very fine ware produced including ornamental and practical pieces. The classic Belleek naturalistic designs were produced by Willits, designs originating from Armstrong at Belleek. Two marks each a twisted serpent in the shape of a "W", one with the word "BELLEEK" above the "W" mark.

5. The Columbian Art Pottery Company founded in 1892 by yet another ex-Belleek potter, W. T. Morris, who had also once worked at the English Worcester factory as well as at Ott and Brewer. He had a partner named F. R. Williams and he also at one time worked at Worcester as a decorator, and at Ott and Brewer. A case of two colleagues teaming up and pooling their skills. Mark, a shield with letters "M" and "W" inside, "Belleek" above on ribbon scroll and "NJ" beneath.

6. The Lenox Corporation. Founded by Walter Lenox in about 1906, he started his potting life as an apprentice with Willits, moving eventually to Ott and Brewer where he rose to be Art Director. Lenox formed a partnership with Jonathan Coxon to found the Ceramic Art Company which traded from 1889 until 1891, when Lenox bought Coxon out and ran the business on his own. He then re-organised the business as Lenox Incorporated, which is still trading and which enjoys a world-wide reputation for fine ceramic ware. Early in his career Lenox was taken ill with paralysis, followed by blindness, and although he could not enjoy the sight of the fine wares produced in his works his business acumen was unimpaired, and with the help of loyal assistants the works prospered.

In the Winterthur Portfolio No. 7 (published for the H. F. du Pont Winterthur Museum by the University Press of Virginia, Charlottesville edited by Ian Quimby), James Mitchell writes at some length and with great authority on the ceramic industry of New Jersey. In this well-researched monograph Mitchell records the history and activities of the Trenton factories which produced a wide range of porcelain, graniteware, creamware and ironstone china. From this fascinating record the following excerpts are of particular interest, touching as they do on the production of American Belleek.

Mr. Mitchell writes, "Throughout its ceramic history America has been an English province, and the late 19th century was no exception especially in the field of high quality porcelain ware, the acme of the potter's art. In the 1870's America produced little true glazed porcelain. England, Ireland and the Continent monopolized the manufacture of glazed translucent ware, and Americans bought it.

In 1876 Ott and Brewer perfected a body they called Ivory Porcelain, and made a new departure in the history of American ceramics. It included kaolin and felspar with small quantities of fritt and ball clay, and was made entirely of American materials".

Mitchell refers, as does Anna Reilly, to the great success enjoyed by Ott and Brewer at the Philadelphia Centennial Exposition and continues "Ott and Brewer's Ivory Porcelain was an attempt to copy porcelain made in Ireland at Belleek, a thin porcelain body of cream colour covered with an iridescent glaze that was labelled nacreous". Mitchell describes in detail the process of making Belleek (the plaster of Paris moulds, the effect of shrinking the ware etc., just as at the present day factory), and states that it is not known whether the ware was glazed before or after the first firing, but that any painted decoration was fired at a second firing, and any gilding in a third firing. "Ott and Brewer continued their efforts to imitate Belleek porcelain until 1883, when Bromley Sr. arrived and true Belleek ware was produced". From this it is clear that the Ott and Brewer Belleek in the Parkfield Collection is post-Bromley, as although rather whiter than contemporary Irish Belleek the thinness and glaze are in every way comparable with the best Irish ware. Mitchell proceeds, "Ott and Brewer continued their policy of advertising their wares at Exhibitions throughout the 1870's and 1880's. Two nacreous glazed Belleek porcelain mirror frames made by Ott and Brewer were exhibited at the New Orleans Exposition of 1884, marked with the O. & B. crescent, and the name of the Exposition. (New Jersey State Museum). Business was good in the late 1880's and in this period Ott and Brewer probably produced the great quantity of (American) Belleek with their mark which has survived to this day".

The Etruria works of Ott and Brewer employed some 250 people in 1887, the power for the machinery being provided by steam engines, unlike the original Belleek works which Armstrong provided with power from the River Erne which flows close to the works. The number of work-people at Ott and Brewer was rather larger than that at Belleek, but it must be remembered that only part of Ott and Brewer's output was of the Belleek type. The factory itself was a raw and unlovely building typical of American industrial architecture of the period, Mitchell describes it as "mainly brick" and "surrounded by various frame sheds". A far cry from the attractive building by Armstrong which he designed for Belleek in Fermanagh (see Fig. 2).

In 1892 a potters' strike together with a slump combined to cause the failure of the business, and the premises were sold to Cook and Co. In his later years Brewer reflected that while the Etruria works may not have been a great financial success it had none the less made a real contribution to the history of ceramics. So ends the fascinating and involved history of the manufacture of Belleek in America. We can count ourselves lucky that the original Irish factory survives to this day, and goes from strength to strength, now exporting some 70% of its output to world markets, the largest single overseas buyer being the United States of America.

With the advent of low priced holidays to the United States, visitors with an interest in ceramics in general, and Belleek in particular, should not fail to visit the New Jersey State Museum, 205, West State St., Trenton, New Jersey, where Mr. Ed Grusheski will prove to be a fund of information.

Recommended reading "The Pottery and Porcelain of the United States" (G. P. Putnam's Sons, c. 1893; 3rd ed. 1909) by Edwin Atlee Barber. Also "Ott and Brewer: Etruria in America" by James Mitchell published by the University Press of Virginia, Charlottesville.

Fig. 7
Ott and Brewer, Crown and Sword mark. Trenton, New Jersey, 1876-1882.

Fig. 8
Ott and Brewer, Crescent mark. Trenton, New Jersey, 1883-1892.

Fig. 9
American Belleek shell bowls, H 2in., W 4in. Ott and Brewer, Trenton, New Jersey. 1883/1892. Parkfield Collection. Crescent mark.

COLLECTIONS WITH EXAMPLES OF BELLEEK

The Parkfield Collection of Belleek Ceramic Art.
Consisting of some 100 or so fine pieces collected by the writer G. M. Smith.

The Victoria and Albert Museum, South Kensington, London.
Three fine pieces in the Main Gallery, but look for the 15 or so pieces housed in the Department of Regional Services on the ground floor.

The Ulster Museum, Belfast.
As the foremost Museum in Northern Ireland. in which the Factory stands, one would expect a grand selection in Belfast. It is here, including statuary. See also Sean McCrum's "The Belleek Pottery" (H.M.S.O.) available from the Museum.

Merseyside County Museum, William Brown St., Liverpool.
Three pieces here, but do ask to see the Belleek Catalogue issued by the Belleek Pottery Ltd. for 1923. This covers what may be called the middle period, much stoneware and general domestic goods were still being made, the earliest models were still going strong as is the case today (1978). Figs. 11, 12, 13, 14 and 15.

City Museum and Art Gallery, Hanley, Stoke on Trent.
The Keeper of Ceramics, Mr. G. W. Elliott, describes their Belleek as "ordinary", perhaps modestly.

City of Birmingham Museum, Congreve St., Birmingham.
A basket and a double handled and double spouted jug with 2nd mark.

Leicester Museum, New Walls, Leicester. One basket.

City of Manchester Museum, Mosley St., Manchester.
A small basket with the usual mark impressed on a small strip fired to the base of the piece. Similar to the small basket in the Parkfield Collection. Four tea cups and saucers, Registry (Diamond) mark for 22nd February 1869, the mark printed in brown.

Glasgow Museum, Kelvingrove, Glasgow.
Five pieces here, including an early sugar bowl with orange jewelling and a rare early mark in dark grey. Also a cup and saucer, jug and tea-pot of the 4th period.

Art Gallery and Museum of the Royal Pavilion, Brighton.
A taper vase of circa 1910 (4th mark) in the form of a shell.

National Museum of Ireland, Kildare St., Dublin.
As may be expected a large and representative collection of all periods, but sadly no published catalogue.

SOME STOCKISTS OF MODERN BELLEEK IN GREAT BRITAIN AND IRELAND

In England

Messrs. Harrods. London.
Selfridges, Oxford St., London.
The Creation Shop, Burlington St., London.
The Irish Shop, Duke St., London.
Ireland House, New Bond St., London.
Lindy Lou, Institute Rd., Swanage, Dorset.

In Ireland

Messrs. Switzers, Dublin.
China Showrooms, Dublin.
Messrs. Weirs, Dublin.
Creation Shops, Dublin.
Messrs. John Meldrum and Sons, Sligo.
Joseph Knox, Waterford.
Irish Crystal Glass, Cork.
Messrs. Stephen Faller & Co., Galway.
Messrs. Austin & Co., Derry.
Cash & Co., Cork.
Stephen Faller & Co., Limerick.
Carraig Donn Industries, Westport.
Robert Hogg & Co., Belfast.

FURTHER READING

Belleek rarely has more than a few lines in the standard ceramic books, so suggestions for further reading are limited. The following books, however, will be very useful for the Belleek collector:—

Illustrated Guide to Victorian Parian China, by Charles and Dorrie Shinn. (Barrie & Jenkins Ltd., London) Copious illustrations, with a very good section on Belleek.

The Observer's Book of Pottery and Porcelain, by Mary and Geoffrey Payton. (Frederick Warne and Co. Ltd., London) One of many "Observer's" books, full of useful information and illustrations of help to the beginner as well as the well-informed.

The Belleek Pottery, by S. McCrum. (HMSO, Ulster Museum, Belfast.) Beautifully produced history of the Belleek factory, particularly fine researching.

Pocket Book of British Ceramic Marks, by J. P. Cushion. (Faber and Faber, London.) No porcelain collector should be without this classic work.

Fig. 10
Senior craftsmen working at the bench in front of Armstrong's high windows watched by the writer's wife. Photograph by the writer.

Fig. 11

Cover of 1923 Catalogue. This and the four following illustrations by courtesy of Merseyside County Museum.

Belleek Pottery Works Co.,

— Limited, —

BELLEEK, CO. FERMANAGH,

IRELAND.

New Illustrated Catalogue

OF

IVORY CHINA,

PARIAN AND EARTHENWARE.

IVORY CHINA AND PARIAN.

BREAKFAST SERVICES,
DESSERT SERVICES,
TEA and AFTERNOON SERVICES,
FIGURES,
FRUIT STANDS,
CENTRE PIECES,

VASES,
FLOWER POTS,
CARD BASKETS,
BISCUIT AND TOBACCO JARS,
SWEET PLATES,
MILK TUMBLERS,

and a General Variety of Fancy Articles suitable for Table, Sideboard, and Mantel Decoration.

EARTHENWARE.

BREAKFAST AND TEA SERVICES,
DINNER SERVICES,
TOILET SERVICES,
MILK PANS
K PANS,
FOOT PANS,

CHAIR PANS,
BED PANS,
PUDDING BOWLS,
BAKING DISHES,
JUGS, MUGS, BOWLS,
AND ALL THE GENERAL LINES OF EARTHENWARE.

ALSO MAKERS OF SANITARY GOODS.

Initials, Crests, and Coats of Arms executed in first-class style.

W & G BAIRD LTD BELFAST

Fig. 12
Title Page 1923 Catalogue.

Fig. 13
Examples of a Belleek "shell" tea service. 1923 Catalogue.

Fig. 14
Examples of Belleek basketware. 1923 Catalogue.

Fig. 15
Examples of Belleek tableware "Shamrock" pattern. 1923 Catalogue.

Fig. 16
Statuette, "Erin Unveiling Her First Pot". Height 17in. Parian body. Apart from harp, cross and some details of drapery, in iridescent glaze. Base of urn inscribed "Belleek Pottery". First mark in black, Belleek Co. Fermanagh impressed. Ulster Museum.

Fig. 17
Parian Bust. "The Clytie." 1st mark 1860. Colour? Writer unable to examine mark. Height 11 inches. V and A.

Fig. 18
Rare tea pot of exceptional quality. 1st mark in black. Parkfield Collection.

Fig. 19
Flower basket of typical design. 4th mark in black. Height overall 4in. Parkfield Collection.

Fig. 20
Miniature Jardiniere 4th mark in black. Height 3in. Parkfield Collection.

Fig. 21
Shell Cup and Saucer 4th mark. A typical Belleek marine pattern. This piece bears the variant of the 4th mark incorporating the name Robinson & Cleaver. Parkfield Collection.

Fig. 22

Jug, height 12in., maximum width of body excluding handle 8in. Earthenware body. Decorated with floral motifs, in panels. In blue on white lead body glaze. Second mark in blue grey. Diamond mark for 5th February 1877. Ulster Museum.

Fig. 23
Thistle Vase. 4th mark in black. Height 8½in. Parkfield Collection.

Fig. 24

Vase decorated with flowers and bird. Note stem in neck of vase

Fig. 25
Modern Belleek mug (c. 1972) 5th mark in green (earlier 5th mark was in black)
Height 3in. (Parkfield Collection)